T0024771

STEP-BY-STEP
Parts of Speech

LINWORTH LEARNING

From the Minds of Teachers

Linworth Publishing, Inc.
Worthington, Ohio

Cataloging-in-Publication Data

Editor: Claire Morris

Design and Production: Good Neighbor Press, Inc.

Published by Linworth Publishing, Inc.
480 East Wilson Bridge Road, Suite L
Worthington, Ohio 43085

Copyright © 2003 by Linworth Publishing, Inc.

All rights reserved. Purchasing this book entitles a librarian to reproduce activity sheets for use in the library within a school or entitles a teacher to reproduce activity sheets for single classroom use within a school. Other portions of the book (up to 15 pages) may be copied for staff development purposes within a single school. Standard citation information should appear on each page. The reproduction of any part of this book for an entire school or school system or for commercial use is strictly prohibited. No part of this book may be electronically reproduced, transmitted, or recorded without written permission from the publisher.

ISBN: 1-58683-148-8

5 4 3

Table of Contents

Nouns

Nouns Name People . . . 1
Nouns Name Places . . . 2
Nouns Name Things . . . 3
More Nouns Name Things . . . 4
Sorting Nouns . . . 5
Plural People, Places, and Things . . . 6
Plural Nouns . . . 7
One or More? . . . 8
Singular and Plural Nouns . . . 9
Reflect and Review . . . 10

Verbs

Identifying Verbs . . . 11
More Identifying Verbs . . . 12
Verbs at Home . . . 13
Verbs in the Kitchen . . . 14
Present Tense Verbs . . . 15
Which Verb? . . . 16
Past Tense Verbs . . . 17
Past Tense Verb Maze . . . 18
Present and Past Tense Verbs . . . 19
Subject-Verb Agreement . . . 20
Matching Nouns and Verbs . . . 21
Choosing the Verb . . . 22
Reflect and Review . . . 23

Articles

Introducing Articles . . . 24
Article Puzzle . . . 25
Articles on a Train . . . 26
A or *An*? . . . 27
Choosing the Article . . . 28
More *A* or *An*? . . . 29
Reflect and Review . . . 30

Assessments

Assessment 1 . . . 31
Assessment 2 . . . 32
Assessment 3 . . . 33
Assessment 4 . . . 34
Assessment 5 . . . 35
Assessment 6 . . . 36
Assessment 7 . . . 37
Assessment 8 . . . 38
Assessment 9 . . . 39

Answer Key . . . 40

Copyright © 2003 Linworth Publishing, Inc.

Introduction

Step-by-Step Parts of Speech is designed to motivate and engage students who may have difficulty with language. Skills are addressed in a variety of fun and interesting formats to accommodate individual learning styles. Each skill is introduced according to a developmental progression and at low readability levels to promote success and understanding. Activity sheets have clear and simple instructions, examples,and exercises which may include word manipulation, understanding pictorial cues, and problem-solving. Assessment activities follow the format of standardized tests and require students to eliminate incorrect options, choose the correct answer, and fill in the appropriate circle. The material in this book correlates with the national curriculum standards for Grades 1–2 and covers the following skills: identifying and correctly using singular and plural nouns, identifying and correctly using present and past tense verbs, and identifying and correctly using articles. An answer key is provided at the back of the book.

Copyright © 2003 Linworth Publishing, Inc.

Name_____ Date_____

Nouns Name People

Directions:
Look at the picture.
Choose the correct noun from the choices below.
Write the word on the line.

People

man girl boy grandma baby

1. grandma

2. _____

3. _____

4. _____

5. _____

Copyright © 2003 Linworth Publishing, Inc.

Name_____ Date_____

Nouns Name Places

Directions:
Look at the map.
Read each question.
Use the map to answer the questions.

1. Where can people find many books? library
2. Where can people play outside? _____
3. Where can people swim? _____
4. Where can people live? _____
5. Where can people go to class? _____
6. Where can people buy something? _____

Copyright © 2003 Linworth Publishing, Inc.

Name_____ Date_____

Nouns Name Things

Directions:
Look at the picture.
Choose the correct noun from the choices below.
Write the word on the line.

Things

mouth ear hair leg foot arm hand nose

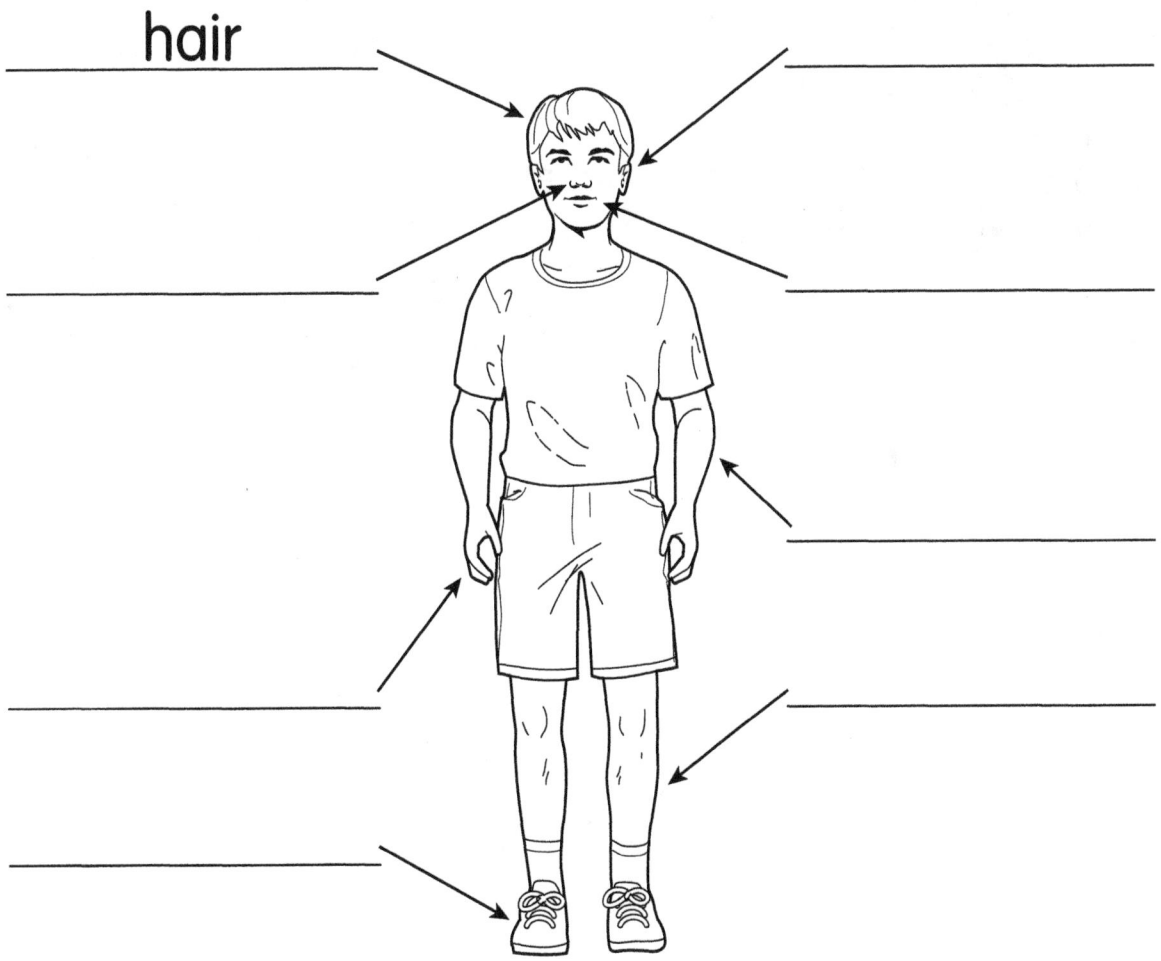

Copyright © 2003 Linworth Publishing, Inc.

Name_____ Date_____

More Nouns Name Things

Directions:
Look at the picture.
Choose the correct noun from the choices below.
Write the word on the line.

Things

ball crab sun boat shell

1. boat

2. _____

3. _____

4. _____

5. _____

Copyright © 2003 Linworth Publishing, Inc.

Name_____ Date_____

Sorting Nouns

Directions:
Read each noun.
Cut out each noun, and glue it in the correct box.

People	Places	Things
boy	street	toy

man

frog

house

park

baby

girl

school

tree

fork

Copyright © 2003 Linworth Publishing, Inc.

Name_____ Date_____

Plural People, Places, and Things

Directions:
Look at the picture.
Write the correct plural noun.
Draw a picture of the plural noun.

1. 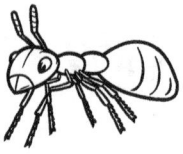 ant + s = ants	
2.  cat + s = _____	
3.  bike + s = _____	
4.  tree + s = _____	
5.  boat + s = _____	

Copyright © 2003 Linworth Publishing, Inc.

Name_____ Date_____

Plural Nouns

Directions:
Read each group of words.
Write the correct plural noun.
Draw a picture of the plural noun.

1. one chick two chicks	
2. one pig three _____	
3. one cow two _____	
4. one dog three _____	
5. one duck four _____	

Copyright © 2003 Linworth Publishing, Inc.

Name_____ Date_____

One or More?

Directions:
Read the grocery list below.
Circle the correct nouns.

We need to buy:

1. four (apple, apples)
2. two (pear, pears)
3. one (banana, bananas)
4. seven (grape, grapes)
5. three (orange, oranges)
6. six (egg, eggs)

Copyright © 2003 Linworth Publishing, Inc.

Name_____ Date_____

Singular and Plural Nouns

Directions:
Look at the picture.
Choose the singular and plural nouns from the choices below.
Write the words in the correct columns.

Nouns

fish crabs cat frog birds dogs

Singular Nouns (Only One)	**Plural Nouns** (More than One)
1. cat	1. _____
2. _____	2. _____
3. _____	3. _____

Copyright © 2003 Linworth Publishing, Inc.

Name_____ Date_____

Reflect and Review

Directions:
Read each sentence.
Circle the singular nouns.
Draw a box around the plural nouns.

1. The (girl) eats two [cookies].
2. The woman reads two books.
3. The dogs bark at the bird.
4. The girls make a kite.
5. The man picks up three bags.
6. The cat plays with the toys.

Copyright © 2003 Linworth Publishing, Inc.

Name_____ Date_____

Identifying Verbs

Directions:
Read each sentence, and look at the picture.
Choose the correct verb from the words below.
Write the word on the line.

Verbs

sings talks bakes jumps drives reads

1. The moose drives.

2. The moose _____.

3. The moose _____.

4. The moose _____.

5. The moose _____.

6. The moose _____.

Copyright © 2003 Linworth Publishing, Inc.

Name_____ Date_____

More Identifying Verbs

Directions:
Look at each group of words.
Color the verb red.
Color the other words yellow.

1.

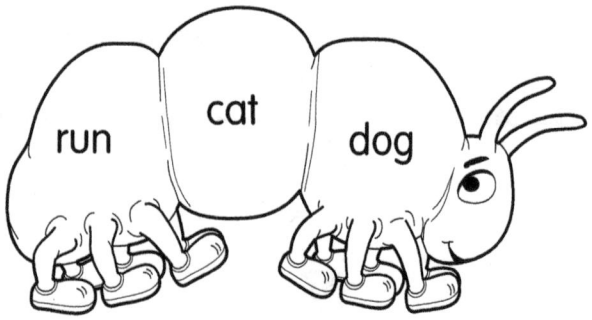

2.

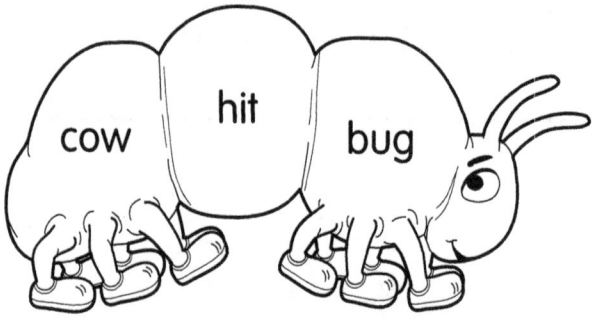

3.

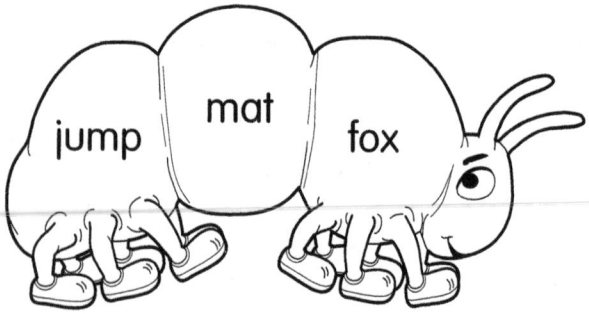

4.

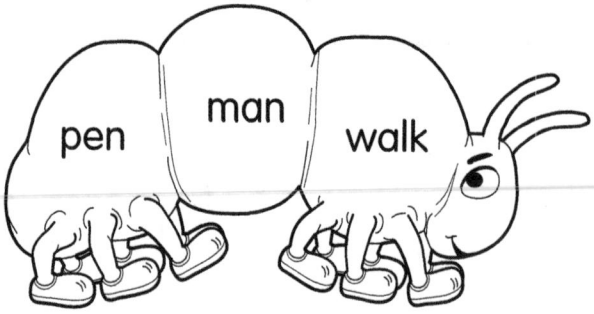

5.

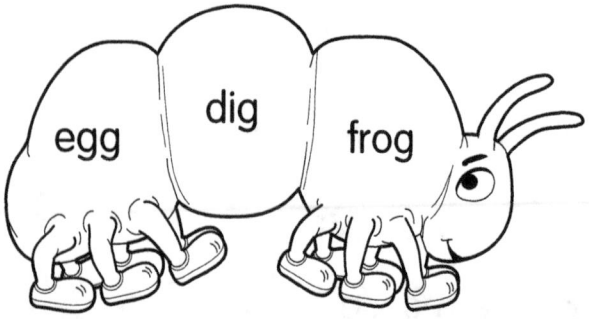

6.

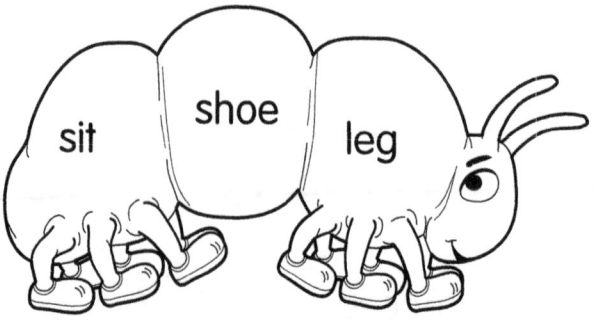

Copyright © 2003 Linworth Publishing, Inc.

Name_____ Date_____

Verbs at Home

Directions:
Look at the picture.
Circle the people who are doing something.
Read each sentence.
Choose the correct verb from the choices below.
Write the word on the line.

Verbs

sweeps mops folds irons

1. The mom sweeps.
2. The girl _____.
3. The boy _____.
4. The dad _____.

Copyright © 2003 Linworth Publishing, Inc.

Name_____ Date_____

Verbs in the Kitchen

Directions:
Read the information below.
Circle the verb in each sentence.
Then, draw a picture of a person making pudding.

How to Make Chocolate Pudding

I open the box of pudding.

I pour the mix into a bowl.

I measure three cups of milk.

I add the milk into the bowl.

I stir the pudding and milk.

I put it in the refrigerator.

I wait for it to cool.

I serve the pudding.

Copyright © 2003 Linworth Publishing, Inc.

Name_____ Date_____

Present Tense Verbs

Directions:
Color the present tense verbs yellow.
Color the other words blue.
Write the verbs in the space below.

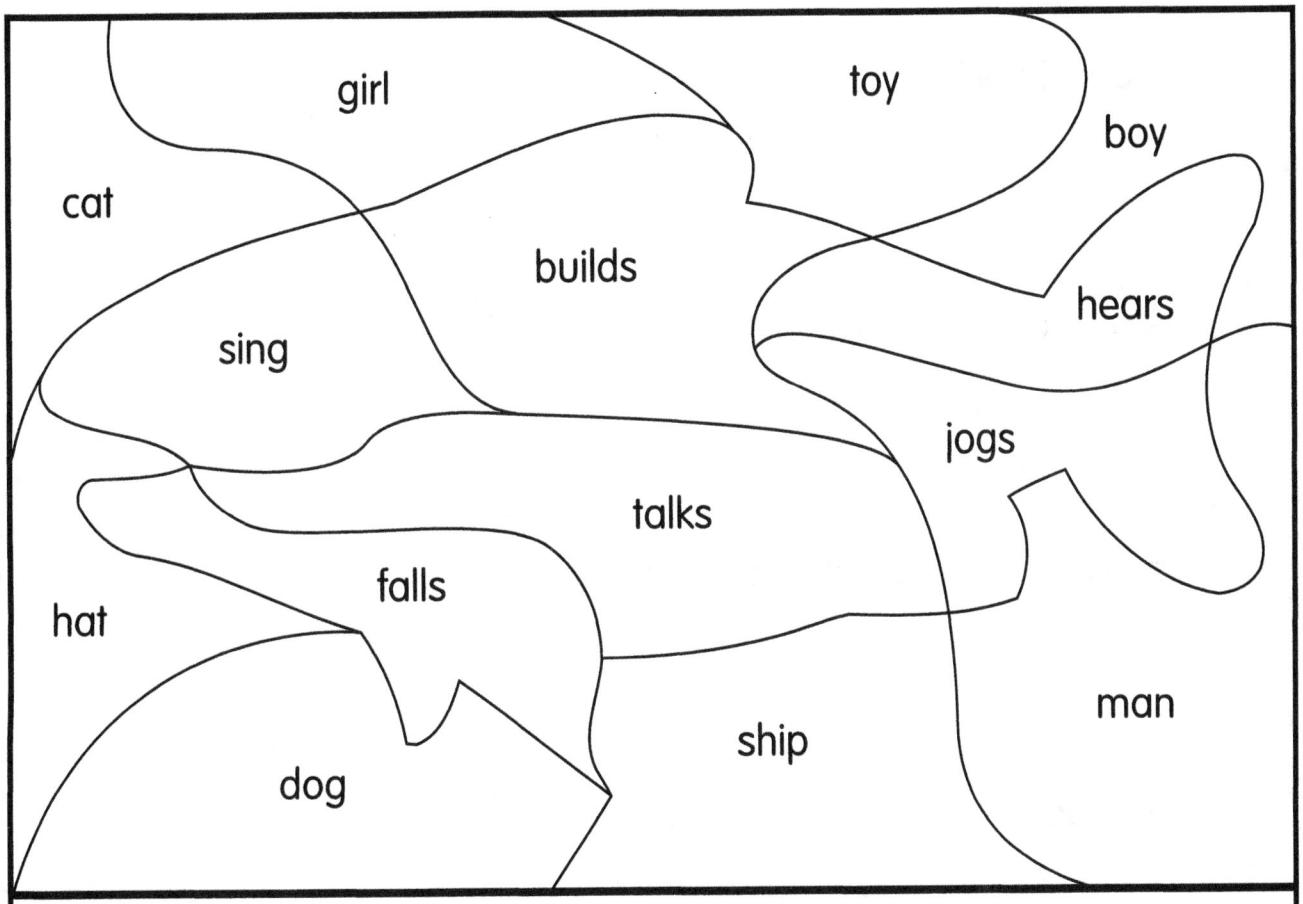

Verbs

sing _____

_____

_____

Copyright © 2003 Linworth Publishing, Inc.

Name_____ Date_____

Which Verb?

Directions:
Read each sentence.
Circle the correct verb.

1. The boy (jump, (jumps)) rope.

2. The girls (throw, throws) the ball.

3. The baby (sleep, sleeps) in the crib.

4. The dogs (run, runs) in the yard.

5. The flowers (grow, grows) in the garden.

6. The cat (sit, sits) in the chair.

Copyright © 2003 Linworth Publishing, Inc.

Name_____ Date_____

Past Tense Verbs

Directions:
Match the shoes.
Draw a line from the present tense shoe to the correct past tense shoe.

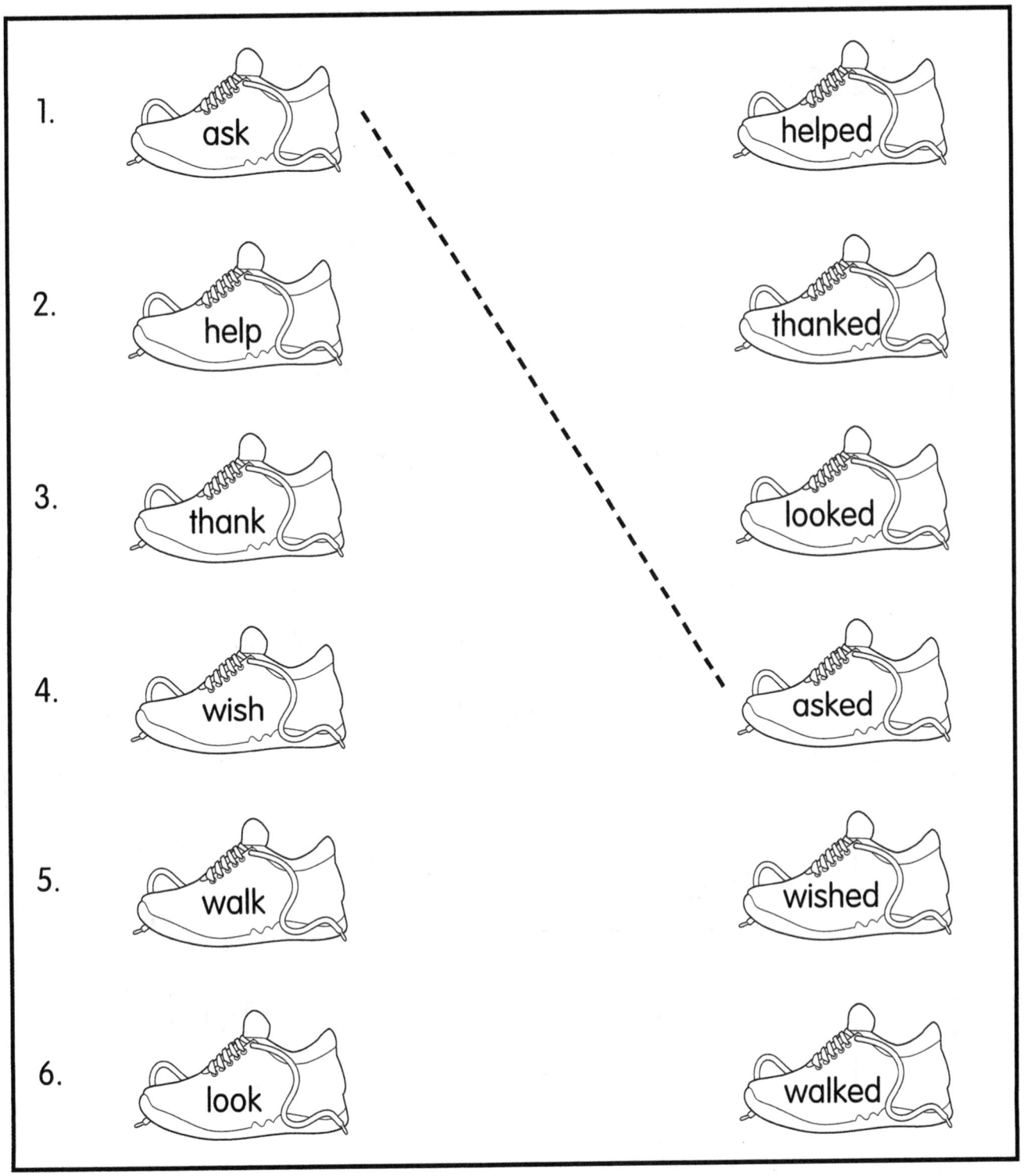

Copyright © 2003 Linworth Publishing, Inc.

Name_____ Date_____

Past Tense Verb Maze

Directions:
Follow the past tense verbs to finish the maze.
Help the baby ant find its family.

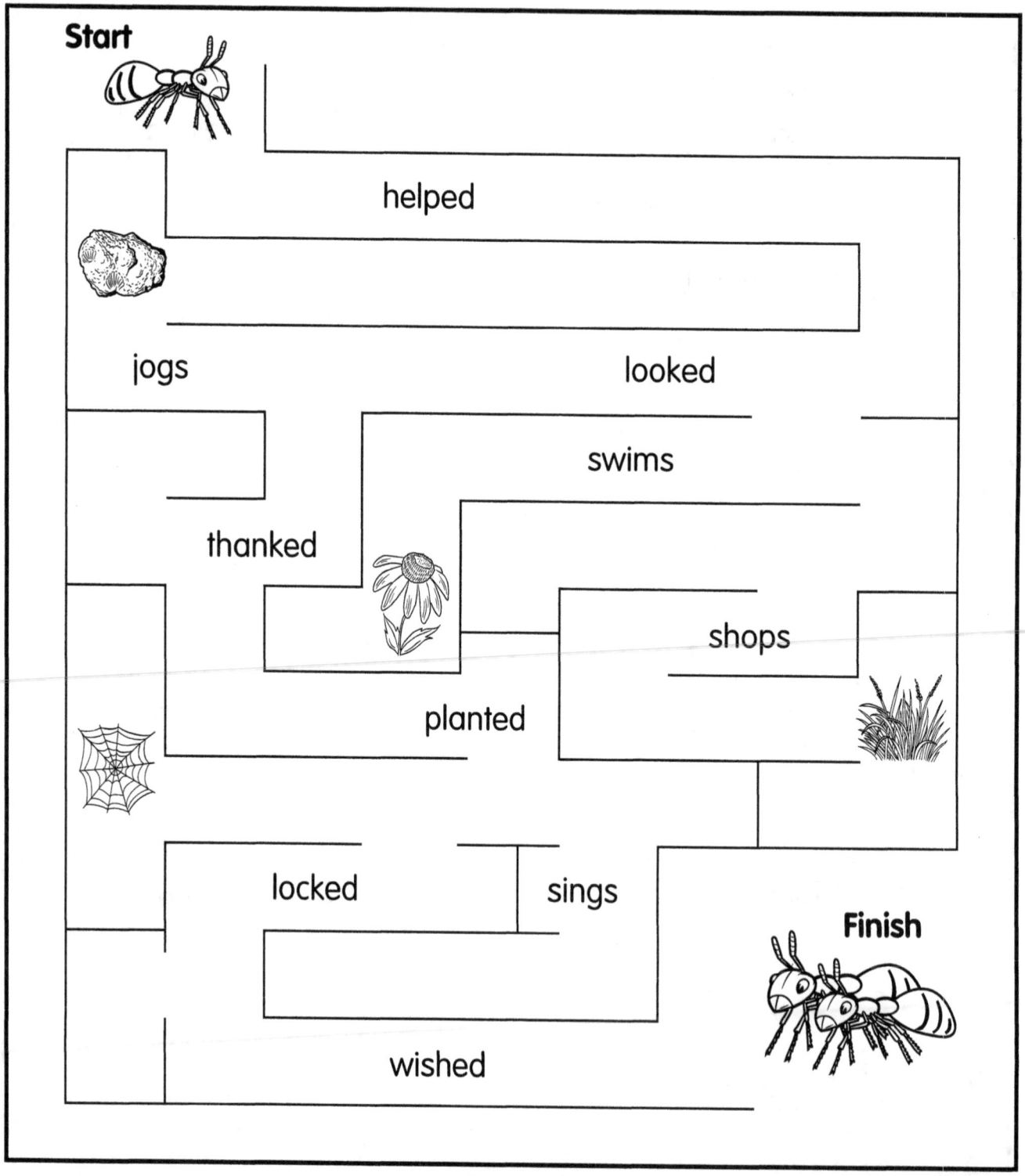

Copyright © 2003 Linworth Publishing, Inc.

Name_____ Date_____

Present and Past Tense Verbs

Directions:
Read each verb, and cut it out.
Decide if it is a present tense or past tense verb.
Glue the verb in the correct box.

Present Tense

Past Tense

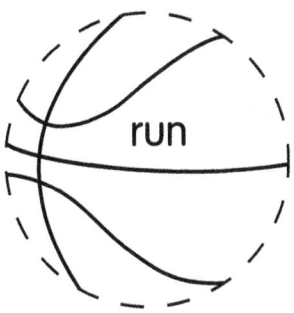

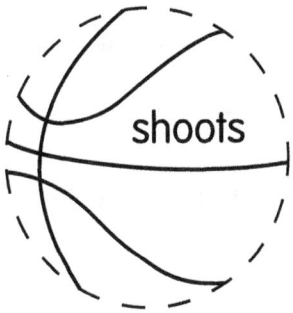

Copyright © 2003 Linworth Publishing, Inc.

Name_____ Date_____

Subject-Verb Agreement

Directions:
Read each sentence, and look at the picture.
Circle the correct verb.

1. The 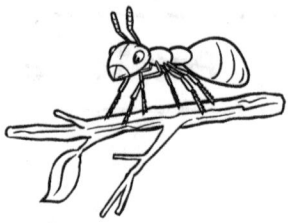 (look, (looks)) for food.

2. The  (play, plays) in the mud.

3. The  (sit, sits) in the nest.

4. The  (eat, eats) hay.

5. The  (climb, climbs) a tree.

Copyright © 2003 Linworth Publishing, Inc.

Name_____ Date_____

Matching Nouns and Verbs

Directions:
Look at the pictures of the nouns, and read each verb.
Draw a line to the correct picture.

1. 

2. 

sing

sings

3. 

hop

4. 

hops

5. 

sleep

6. 

sleeps

Copyright © 2003 Linworth Publishing, Inc.

Name_____ Date_____

Choosing the Verb

Directions:
Look at the pictures of the nouns, and read each verb.
Circle the correct verb.

1.		sing sings
2.		shine shines
3.		bark barks
4.		swim swims
5.		eat eats
6.		sleep sleeps

Copyright © 2003 Linworth Publishing, Inc.

Name_____ Date_____

Reflect and Review

Directions:
Read each group of words.
Decide whether the group of words is a sentence.
If it is a sentence, circle yes.
Then, underline the nouns and circle the verb.
If it is not a sentence, circle no.

1. Yes No The girls play.

2. Yes No The boys.

3. Yes No The baby takes a nap.

4. Yes No The woman reads a book.

5. Yes No Runs to the house.

6. Yes No My friend sings.

Copyright © 2003 Linworth Publishing, Inc.

Name_____ Date_____

Introducing Articles

Directions:
Read the poem.
Circle the articles.
Then, write the articles on the lines below.

There was (an) old woman

who swallowed a fly.

I don't know why

she swallowed the fly.

I think she'll cry!

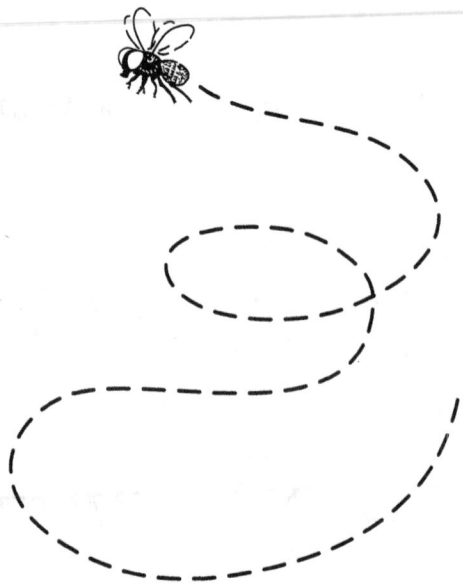

1. an

2. _____

3. _____

Copyright © 2003 Linworth Publishing, Inc.

Name_____ Date_____

Article Puzzle

Directions:
Read each word.
If the word is an article, color the puzzle piece blue.
If the word is not an article, color the puzzle piece yellow.
Write the articles in the space below.

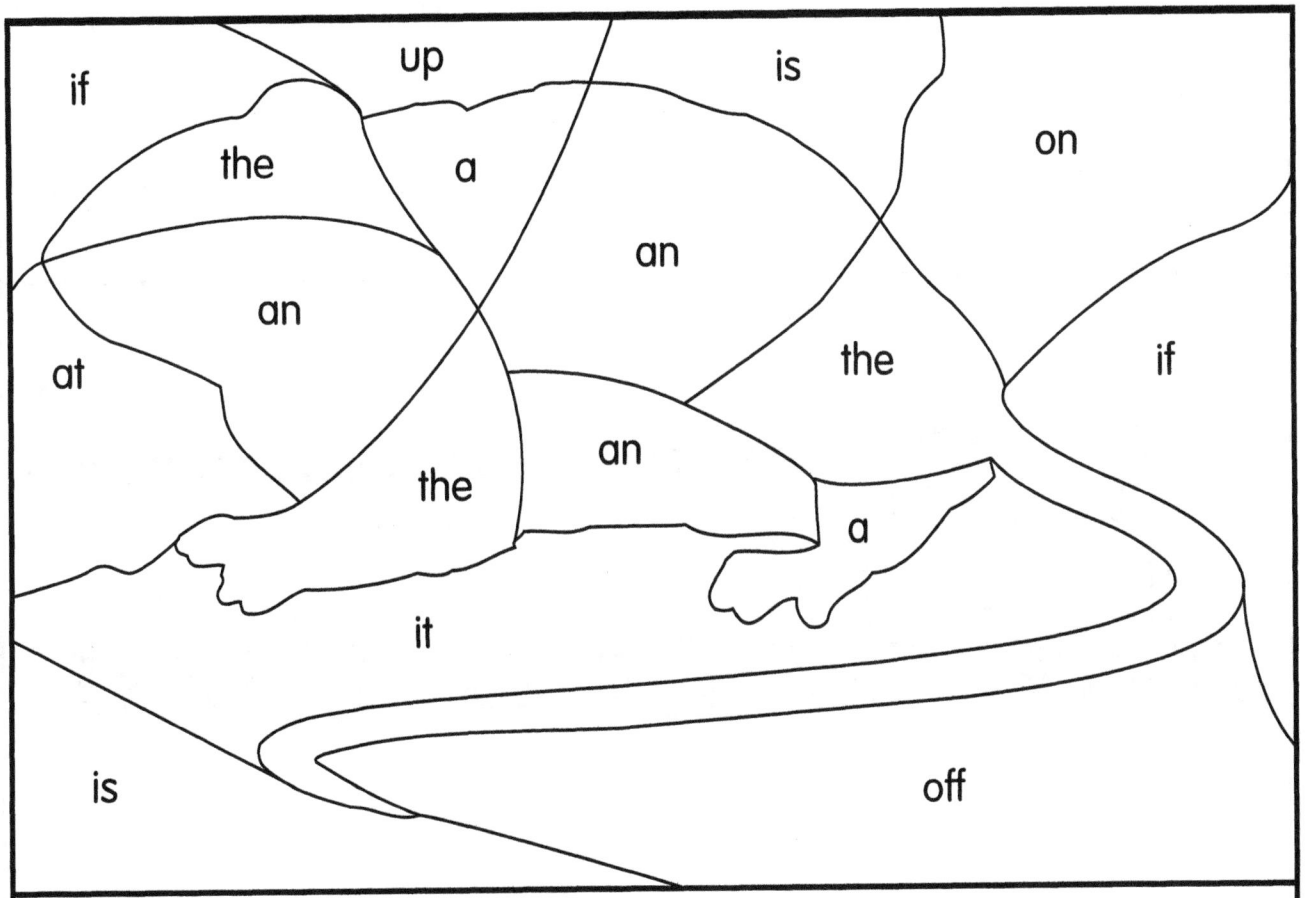

Articles

the _____

_____

_____

Copyright © 2003 Linworth Publishing, Inc.

Name_____ Date_____

Articles on a Train

Directions:
Read each word.
Write each word on a train car.
If the word is an article, color the train car yellow.
If the word is not an article, color the train car red.

Word box

a at of an the

Copyright © 2003 Linworth Publishing, Inc.

Name_____ Date_____

A or *An*?

Directions:
Look at each picture, and say what the picture is.
If the word begins with a consonant sound, write ***a***.
If the word begins with a vowel sound, write ***an***.

1. a

2. _____

3. _____

4. _____

5. _____

6. _____

Copyright © 2003 Linworth Publishing, Inc.

Name_____ Date_____

Choosing the Article

Directions:
Look at the pictures in each box.
Circle the pictures that use the article.

a

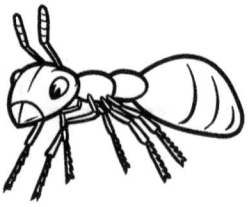

an

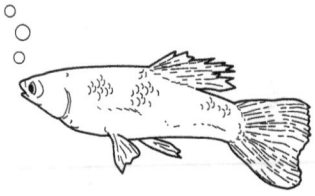

Copyright © 2003 Linworth Publishing, Inc.

Name_____ Date_____

More *A* or *An*?

Directions:
Read each sentence.
Circle the correct article.

1. My friend bakes (a, an) cake.

2. She adds (a, an) egg.

3. She pours (a, an) cup of milk in the bowl.

4. She stirs the batter with (a, an) spoon.

5. She puts it in (a, an) pan.

6. She bakes the cake in (a, an) oven.

Copyright © 2003 Linworth Publishing, Inc.

Name_____ Date_____

Reflect and Review

Directions:
Read each noun.
Circle the correct article for each noun.
If the noun names only one, underline the noun once.
If the noun names more than one, underline the noun twice.

1. (the, and) dogs	
2. (a, an) ant	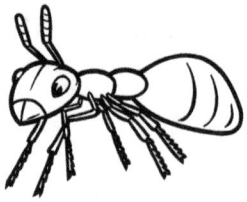
3. (a, an) pig	
4. (a, an) tree	
5. (a, an) owl	
6. (a, the) flowers	

Copyright © 2003 Linworth Publishing, Inc.

Name_____ Date_____

Assessment 1

Directions:
Read each group of words.
Fill in the circle next to the noun.

1. ○ jump
   ○ climb
   ● boy

2. ○ girl
   ○ sing
   ○ play

3. ○ jog
   ○ walk
   ○ boy

4. ○ car
   ○ drive
   ○ say

5. ○ swim
   ○ sleep
   ○ house

Copyright © 2003 Linworth Publishing, Inc.

Name_____ Date_____

Assessment 2

Directions:
Read each question.
Fill in the circle next to the correct answer.

1. Which noun names a place?

girl	fan	store
○	○	●

2. Which noun names a person?

frog	town	man
○	○	○

3. Which noun names a thing?

boy	dog	baby
○	○	○

4. Which noun names a place?

room	bed	toy
○	○	○

5. Which noun names a person?

house	pool	lady
○	○	○

6. Which noun names a thing?

bike	park	grandpa
○	○	○

Copyright © 2003 Linworth Publishing, Inc.

Name_____ Date_____

Assessment 3

Directions:
Look at each picture.
Read each group of words.
Fill in the circle next to the correct answer.

1.		○ cat ● cats
2.		○ bike ○ bikes
3.	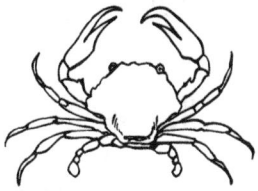	○ crab ○ crabs
4.	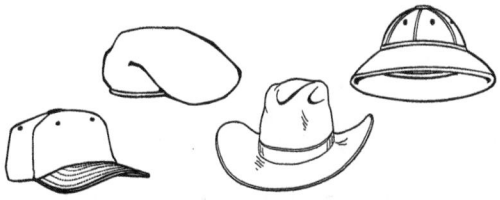	○ hat ○ hats
5.		○ school ○ schools
6.		○ tree ○ trees

Copyright © 2003 Linworth Publishing, Inc.

Name_____ Date_____

Assessment 4

Directions:
Read each sentence.
Fill in the circle next to the correct answer.

1. The boy has two	○ book. ● books.
2. The dog finds one	○ bone. ○ bones.
3. The girl picks three	○ flower. ○ flowers.
4. The baby plays with one	○ toy. ○ toys.
5. The cat had two	○ kitten. ○ kittens.
6. The man has six	○ rock. ○ rocks.

Copyright © 2003 Linworth Publishing, Inc.

Name_____ Date_____

Assessment 5

Directions:
Read each group of words.
Fill in the circle for the verb.

1.	○ kit	● hit	○ mitt
2.	○ bake	○ cake	○ lake
3.	○ jog	○ log	○ frog
4.	○ clip	○ lip	○ skip
5.	○ throw	○ bow	○ crow

Copyright © 2003 Linworth Publishing, Inc.

Name_____ Date_____

Assessment 6

Directions:
Read each sentence.
Fill in the circle next to the correct answer.

1. 	Her cat _____ in the yard.	○ yells ○ swims ● runs
2. 	The boy _____ for a snack.	○ looks ○ hides ○ runs
3. 	He _____ a cookie.	○ tells ○ walks ○ eats
4. 	The cat _____ in her lap.	○ talks ○ sleeps ○ stands
5. 	His dad _____ him cookies.	○ bakes ○ jumps ○ sits

Copyright © 2003 Linworth Publishing, Inc.

Name_____ Date_____

Assessment 7

Directions:
Read each sentence.
Fill in the circle next to the correct answer.

1.		He _____ the dog.	○ kicked ○ played ● walked
2.		She _____ the soccer ball.	○ yelled ○ parked ○ kicked
3.		She _____ to her grandma.	○ packed ○ talked ○ climbed
4.		He _____ up shells.	○ picked ○ jumped ○ walked
5.		She _____ a flower.	○ barked ○ smelled ○ blocked

Copyright © 2003 Linworth Publishing, Inc.

Name_____ Date_____

Assessment 8

Directions:
Look at each picture.
Fill in the circle under the correct article.

1.	a ○	an ●	
2.	a ○	an ○	
3.	a ○	an ○	
4.	a ○	an ○	
5.	a ○	an ○	
6.	a ○	an ○	

Copyright © 2003 Linworth Publishing, Inc.

Name_____ Date_____

Assessment 9

Directions:
Read each nursery rhyme.
Circle the articles in each rhyme.

1. Little Miss Muffet
   Sat on (a) tuffet.

2. One, two buckle my shoe,
   Three, four shut the door.

3. Humpty Dumpty sat on a wall.
   Humpty Dumpty had a great fall.

4. There was an old who man
   Who lived in a shoe.

5. And the cow jumped over the moon.
   And the dish ran away with the spoon.

Copyright © 2003 Linworth Publishing, Inc.

Answer Key pages 1–9

Name_____ Date_____

Nouns Name People

Directions:
Look at the picture.
Choose the correct noun from the choices below.
Write the word on the line.

People
man girl boy grandma baby

1. grandma
2. girl
3. baby
4. man
5. boy

Copyright © 2003 Linworth Publishing, Inc.

Name_____ Date_____

Nouns Name Places

Directions:
Look at the map.
Read each question.
Use the map to answer the questions.

1. Where can people find many books? library
2. Where can people play outside? park
3. Where can people swim? pool
4. Where can people live? house
5. Where can people go to class? school
6. Where can people buy something? store

Copyright © 2003 Linworth Publishing, Inc.

Name_____ Date_____

Nouns Name Things

Directions:
Look at the picture.
Choose the correct noun from the choices below.
Write the word on the line.

Things
mouth ear hair leg foot arm hand nose

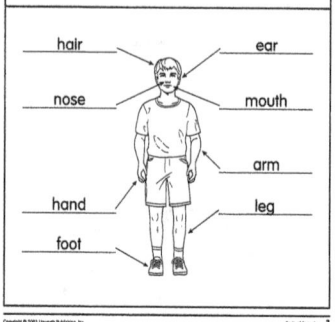

Copyright © 2003 Linworth Publishing, Inc.

Name_____ Date_____

More Nouns Name Things

Directions:
Look at the picture.
Choose the correct noun from the choices below.
Write the word on the line.

Things
ball crab sun boat shell

1. boat
2. ball
3. sun
4. shell
5. crab

Copyright © 2003 Linworth Publishing, Inc.

Name_____ Date_____

Sorting Nouns

Directions:
Read each noun.
Cut out each noun, and glue it in the correct box.

People	Places	Things
boy	street	toy
man	park	tree
baby	school	frog
girl	house	fork

man frog house
park baby girl
school tree fork

Copyright © 2003 Linworth Publishing, Inc.

Name_____ Date_____

Plural People, Places, and Things

Directions:
Look at the picture.
Write the correct plural noun.
Draw a picture of the plural noun.

1.	ant + s = ants	
2.	cat + s = cats	
3.	bike + s = bikes	
4.	tree + s = trees	
5.	boat + s = boats	

Copyright © 2003 Linworth Publishing, Inc.

Name_____ Date_____

Plural Nouns

Directions:
Read each group of words.
Write the correct plural noun.
Draw a picture of the plural noun.

1. one chick	two chicks	
2. one pig	three pigs	
3. one cow	two cows	
4. one dog	three dogs	
5. one duck	four ducks	

Copyright © 2003 Linworth Publishing, Inc.

Name_____ Date_____

One or More?

Directions:
Read the grocery list below.
Circle the correct nouns.

We need to buy:

1. four (apple, apples)
2. two (pear, pears)
3. one (banana, bananas)
4. seven (grape, grapes)
5. three (orange, oranges)
6. six (egg, eggs)

Copyright © 2003 Linworth Publishing, Inc.

Name_____ Date_____

Singular and Plural Nouns

Directions:
Look at the picture.
Choose the singular and plural nouns from the choices below.
Write the words in the correct columns.

Nouns
fish crabs cat frog birds dogs

Singular Nouns (Only One)	Plural Nouns (More than One)
1. cat	1. birds
2. fish	2. dogs
3. frog	3. crabs

Copyright © 2003 Linworth Publishing, Inc.

Copyright © 2003 Linworth Publishing, Inc.

Answer Key pages 10–18

Name_____ Date_____

Reflect and Review

Directions:
Read each sentence.
Circle the singular nouns.
Draw a box around the plural nouns.

1. The (girl) eats two [cookies].
2. The (woman) reads two [books].
3. The [dogs] bark at the (bird).
4. The [girls] make a (kite).
5. The (man) picks up three [bags].
6. The (cat) plays with the [toys].

10 Parts of Speech Copyright © 2003 Linworth Publishing, Inc.

Name_____ Date_____

Identifying Verbs

Directions:
Read each sentence, and look at the picture.
Choose the correct verb from the words below.
Write the word on the line.

Verbs
sings talks bakes jumps drives reads

1. The moose drives.
2. The moose reads.
3. The moose jumps.
4. The moose sings.
5. The moose talks.
6. The moose bakes.

Copyright © 2003 Linworth Publishing, Inc. Parts of Speech 11

Name_____ Date_____

More Identifying Verbs

Directions:
Look at each group of words.
Color the verb red.
Color the other words yellow.

1. red yellow yellow — run cat dog
2. yellow red yellow — cow hit bug
3. red yellow yellow — jump mat fox
4. yellow yellow red — pen man walk
5. yellow red yellow — egg dig frog
6. red yellow yellow — sit shoe leg

12 Parts of Speech Copyright © 2003 Linworth Publishing, Inc.

Name_____ Date_____

Verbs at Home

Directions:
Look at the picture.
Circle the people who are doing something.
Read each sentence.
Choose the correct verb from the choices below.
Write the word on the line.

Verbs
sweeps mops folds irons

1. The mom sweeps.
2. The girl irons.
3. The boy folds.
4. The dad mops.

Copyright © 2003 Linworth Publishing, Inc. Parts of Speech 13

Name_____ Date_____

Verbs in the Kitchen

Directions:
Read the information below.
Circle the verb in each sentence.
Then, draw a picture of a person making pudding.

How to Make Chocolate Pudding

I (open) the box of pudding.
I (pour) the mix into a bowl.
I (measure) three cups of milk.
I (add) the milk into the bowl.
I (stir) the pudding and milk.
I (put) it in the refrigerator.
I (wait) for it to cool.
I (serve) the pudding.

14 Parts of Speech Copyright © 2003 Linworth Publishing, Inc.

Name_____ Date_____

Present Tense Verbs

Directions:
Color the present tense verbs yellow.
Color the other words blue.
Write the verbs in the space below.

blue girl toy blue boy cat blue blue yellow sing builds yellow yellow hears yellow jogs yellow talks hat blue falls yellow blue dog ship man blue blue

Verbs
sing, hears, falls, talks, jogs, builds

Copyright © 2003 Linworth Publishing, Inc. Parts of Speech 15

Name_____ Date_____

Which Verb?

Directions:
Read each sentence.
Circle the correct verb.

1. The boy (jump, (jumps)) rope.
2. The girls ((throw), throws) the ball.
3. The baby (sleep, (sleeps)) in the crib.
4. The dogs ((run), runs) in the yard.
5. The flowers ((grow), grows) in the garden.
6. The cat (sit, (sits)) in the chair.

16 Parts of Speech Copyright © 2003 Linworth Publishing, Inc.

Name_____ Date_____

Past Tense Verbs

Directions:
Match the shoes.
Draw a line from the present tense shoe to the correct past tense shoe.

1. ask — asked
2. help — helped
3. thank — thanked
4. wish — wished
5. walk — walked
6. look — looked

Copyright © 2003 Linworth Publishing, Inc. Parts of Speech 17

Name_____ Date_____

Past Tense Verb Maze

Directions:
Follow the past tense verbs to finish the maze.
Help the baby ant find its family.

Start — helped — looked — swims — shops — planted — sings — Finish — wished — locked — thanked — jogs

18 Parts of Speech Copyright © 2003 Linworth Publishing, Inc.

Copyright © 2003 Linworth Publishing, Inc.

Answer Key pages 19–27

Name_____ Date_____

Present and Past Tense Verbs

Directions:
Read each verb, and cut it out.
Decide if it is a present tense or past tense verb.
Glue the verb in the correct box.

Present Tense	Past Tense
run shoots throws	played helped jumped

run, played, jumped, throws, shoots, helped

Copyright © 2003 Linworth Publishing, Inc.

Name_____ Date_____

Subject-Verb Agreement

Directions:
Read each sentence, and look at the picture.
Circle the correct verb.

1. The (look, looks) for food.
2. The (play, plays) in the mud.
3. The (sit, sits) in the nest.
4. The (eat, eats) hay.
5. The (climb, climbs) a tree.

Copyright © 2003 Linworth Publishing, Inc.

Name_____ Date_____

Matching Nouns and Verbs

Directions:
Look at the pictures of the nouns, and read each verb.
Draw a line to the correct picture.

1. sing
2. sings
3. hop
4. hops
5. sleep
6. sleeps

Copyright © 2003 Linworth Publishing, Inc.

Name_____ Date_____

Choosing the Verb

Directions:
Look at the pictures of the nouns, and read each verb.
Circle the correct verb.

1. sing / sings
2. shine / shines
3. bark / barks
4. swim / swims
5. eat / eats
6. sleep / sleeps

Copyright © 2003 Linworth Publishing, Inc.

Name_____ Date_____

Reflect and Review

Directions:
Read each group of words.
Decide whether the group of words is a sentence.
If it is a sentence, circle yes.
Then, underline the nouns and circle the verb.
If it is not a sentence, circle no.

1. Yes No The girls play.
2. Yes No The boys.
3. Yes No The baby takes a nap.
4. Yes No The woman reads a book.
5. Yes No Runs to the house.
6. Yes No My friend sings.

Copyright © 2003 Linworth Publishing, Inc.

Name_____ Date_____

Introducing Articles

Directions:
Read the poem.
Circle the articles.
Then, write the articles on the lines below.

There was an old woman
who swallowed a fly.
I don't know why
she swallowed the fly.
I think she'll cry!

1. an
2. a
3. the

Copyright © 2003 Linworth Publishing, Inc.

Name_____ Date_____

Article Puzzle

Directions:
Read each word.
If the word is an article, color the puzzle piece blue.
If the word is not an article, color the puzzle piece yellow.
Write the articles in the space below.

if yellow up is yellow the a blue on an blue an at the if yellow the an blue blue a it yellow is yellow off yellow

Articles

the, a, an

Copyright © 2003 Linworth Publishing, Inc.

Name_____ Date_____

Articles on a Train

Directions:
Read each word.
Write each word on a train car.
If the word is an article, color the train car yellow.
If the word is not an article, color the train car red.

Word box

a at of an the

yellow a | red at | red of | yellow an | yellow the

Copyright © 2003 Linworth Publishing, Inc.

Name_____ Date_____

A or *An*?

Directions:
Look at each picture, and say what the picture is.
If the word begins with a consonant sound, write *a*.
If the word begins with a vowel sound, write *an*.

1. a
2. an
3. an
4. an
5. a
6. an

Copyright © 2003 Linworth Publishing, Inc.

Copyright © 2003 Linworth Publishing, Inc.

Answer Key pages 28–36

Name_____ Date_____

Choosing the Article

Directions:
Look at the pictures in each box.
Circle the pictures that use the article.

a

an

28 Parts of Speech

Copyright © 2003 Linworth Publishing, Inc.

Name_____ Date_____

More *A* or *An*?

Directions:
Read each sentence.
Circle the correct article.

1. My friend bakes (a), an) cake.
2. She adds (a, (an) egg.
3. She pours (a), an) cup of milk in the bowl.
4. She stirs the batter with (a), an) spoon.
5. She puts it in (a), an) pan.
6. She bakes the cake in (a, (an) oven.

Copyright © 2003 Linworth Publishing, Inc.

Parts of Speech 29

Name_____ Date_____

Reflect and Review

Directions:
Read each noun.
Circle the correct article for each noun.
If the noun names only one, underline the noun once.
If the noun names more than one, underline the noun twice.

1. (the), and) dogs
2. (a, (an) ant
3. (a), an) pig
4. (a), an) tree
5. (a, (an) owl
6. (a, (the) flowers

30 Parts of Speech

Copyright © 2003 Linworth Publishing, Inc.

Name_____ Date_____

Assessment 1

Directions:
Read each group of words.
Fill in the circle next to the noun.

1. ○ jump
   ○ climb
   ● boy
2. ● girl
   ○ sing
   ○ play
3. ○ jog
   ○ walk
   ● boy
4. ● car
   ○ drive
   ○ say
5. ○ swim
   ○ sleep
   ● house

Copyright © 2003 Linworth Publishing, Inc.

Parts of Speech 31

Name_____ Date_____

Assessment 2

Directions:
Read each question.
Fill in the circle next to the correct answer.

	girl	fan	store
1. Which noun names a place?	○	○	●
2. Which noun names a person?	frog	town	man
	○	○	●
3. Which noun names a thing?	boy	dog	baby
	○	●	○
4. Which noun names a place?	room	bed	toy
	●	○	○
5. Which noun names a person?	house	pool	lady
	○	○	●
6. Which noun names a thing?	bike	park	grandpa
	●	○	○

32 Parts of Speech

Copyright © 2003 Linworth Publishing, Inc.

Name_____ Date_____

Assessment 3

Directions:
Look at each picture.
Read each group of words.
Fill in the circle next to the correct answer.

1. ○ cat
   ● cats
2. ● bike
   ○ bikes
3. ● crab
   ○ crabs
4. ○ hat
   ● hats
5. ● school
   ○ schools
6. ○ tree
   ● trees

Copyright © 2003 Linworth Publishing, Inc.

Parts of Speech 33

Name_____ Date_____

Assessment 4

Directions:
Read each sentence.
Fill in the circle next to the correct answer.

1. The boy has two
   ○ book.
   ● books.
2. The dog finds one
   ● bone.
   ○ bones.
3. The girl picks three
   ○ flower.
   ● flowers.
4. The baby plays with one
   ● toy.
   ○ toys.
5. The cat had two
   ○ kitten.
   ● kittens.
6. The man has six
   ○ rock.
   ● rocks.

34 Parts of Speech

Copyright © 2003 Linworth Publishing, Inc.

Name_____ Date_____

Assessment 5

Directions:
Read each group of words.
Fill in the circle for the verb.

1.	○ kit	● hit	○ mitt
2.	● bake	○ cake	○ lake
3.	● jog	○ log	○ frog
4.	○ clip	○ lip	● skip
5.	● throw	○ bow	○ crow

Copyright © 2003 Linworth Publishing, Inc.

Parts of Speech 35

Name_____ Date_____

Assessment 6

Directions:
Read each sentence.
Fill in the circle next to the correct answer.

1. Her cat _____ in the yard.
   ○ yells
   ○ swims
   ● runs
2. The boy _____ for a snack.
   ● looks
   ○ hides
   ○ runs
3. He _____ a cookie.
   ○ tells
   ○ walks
   ● eats
4. The cat _____ in her lap.
   ○ talks
   ● sleeps
   ○ stands
5. His dad _____ him cookies.
   ● bakes
   ○ jumps
   ○ sits

36 Parts of Speech

Copyright © 2003 Linworth Publishing, Inc.

Copyright © 2003 Linworth Publishing, Inc.

Answer Key pages 37–39

Name_____ Date_____

Assessment 7

Directions:
Read each sentence.
Fill in the circle next to the correct answer.

1.	He _____ the dog.	○ kicked ○ played ● walked
2.	She _____ the soccer ball.	○ yelled ○ parked ● kicked
3.	She _____ to her grandma.	○ packed ● talked ○ climbed
4.	He _____ up shells.	● picked ○ jumped ○ walked
5.	She _____ a flower.	○ barked ● smelled ○ blocked

Copyright © 2003 Linworth Publishing, Inc.

Name_____ Date_____

Assessment 8

Directions:
Look at each picture.
Fill in the circle under the correct article.

	a	an	
1.	○	●	
2.	●	○	
3.	○	●	
4.	○	●	
5.	●	○	
6.	●	○	

Copyright © 2003 Linworth Publishing, Inc.

Name_____ Date_____

Assessment 9

Directions:
Read each nursery rhyme.
Circle the articles in each rhyme.

1. Little Miss Muffet
   Sat on (a) tuffet.
2. One, two buckle my shoe,
   Three, four shut (the) door.
3. Humpty Dumpty sat on (a) wall.
   Humpty Dumpty had (a) great fall.
4. There was (an) old who man
   Who lived in (a) shoe.
5. And (the) cow jumped over (the) moon.
   And (the) dish ran away with (the) spoon.

Copyright © 2003 Linworth Publishing, Inc.

Copyright © 2003 Linworth Publishing, Inc.

Printed in the USA
CPSIA information can be obtained
at www.ICGtesting.com
LVHW080724170724
785510LV00007B/295

9 781586 831486